THE PLACE OF PRAYER

THE PLACE OF PRAYER

Dr. Samuel D. Abbott

Destiny & Victory Publishing

THE PLACE OF PRAYER

Copyright © 2024 by Dr. Samuel D. Abbott

All rights reserved. No part of this book may be reproduced or transmitted in any form or by any means without written permission from the author.

All scripture quotations, unless otherwise indicated are taken from the King James Bible Version.

ISBN: 978-1-962008-13-6

Printed in the United States of America

Published by Destiny & Victory Publishing

Table of Contents

PROLOGUE 1

Chapter 1: PRAYER IS 3

Chapter 2: PLACE OF TRANSFORMATION 7

Chapter 3: PLACE OF SUBMISSION 15

Chapter 4: PLACE OF PREPARATION 23

Chapter 5: PLACE OF REVELATION 27

Chapter 6: A PLACE OF DECISION 33

Chapter 7: A PLACE OF SUPERNATURAL PROTECTION 41

Chapter 8: A PLACE OF DIVINE ORCHESTRATION 45

Chapter 9: A PLACE OF DELIVERANCE 49

Chapter 10: A PLACE OF FAITH 53

ABOUT THE AUTHOR: 57

PROLOGUE

On June 25, 1962, the U.S. Supreme Court made a landmark decision, removing government-endorsed prayer from public schools, deeming the practice unconstitutional. In the wake of this ruling, anecdotes emerged, illustrating the impact of this change. One such story recounts a pupil in a classroom who, upon hearing her teacher sneeze, instinctively uttered, "God bless you." The teacher's response, "Cut that out or we'll both be in trouble," underscores the shift in the educational landscape.

As discussions ensued about the removal of prayer from schools, voices emerged expressing concerns and opinions. One individual lamented, "Now that there's no more praying in schools, kids will have to go to motels to read the Bible. And if this keeps up, the Gideons will have to go underground." In a similar vein, commentator Rush Limbaugh remarked, "Banning prayer in school in effect made God unconstitutional."

Amidst these debates, the sanctity of prayer remains intact within the confines of most churches, still embraced as both constitutional and legal. Yet, one cannot help but ponder why prayer is practiced so sparingly. What significance does prayer hold in our lives? Jonathan Edwards offers insight, asserting, "Prayer is as natural an expression of faith as breathing is of life." Indeed, prayer should seamlessly integrate into our daily routines, much like the act of breathing.

THE PLACE OF PRAYER

Elizabeth George aptly describes prayer as a "secret weapon" that restores our trust in God, while Corrie Ten Boom poses a thought-provoking question: "Is prayer your steering wheel or your spare tire?" In essence, do we engage in prayer merely in times of crisis, or do we allow it to guide our every step?

As you embark on this journey through the pages of this book, my hope and prayer are that you gain a deeper understanding of prayer—a realization that ignites a fervent desire to dwell in the sacred realm of prayer.

CHAPTER 1
PRAYER IS

*"Prayer, as a one-dimensional,
self-centered practice, will surely be unfulfilled."*

How Praying Hyde Prayed

Dr. Wilbur Chapman wrote to a friend:

"I have learned some great lessons concerning prayer. At one of our missions in England, the audience was exceedingly small; but I received a note saying that an American missionary was going to pray for God's blessing down on our work. He was known as Praying Hyde. Almost instantly the tide turned. The hall became packed, and at my first invitation fifty men accepted Christ as their Savior. As we were leaving, I said, 'Mr. Hyde, I want you to pray for me.' He came to my room, turned the key in the door, and dropped on his knees, and waited five minutes without a single syllable coming from his lips. I could hear my own heart thumping, and his beating. I felt hot tears running down my face. I knew I was with God. Then, with upturned face, down which the tears were streaming, he said, 'O God!' Then for five minutes at least he was still again; and then, when he knew that he was talking with God there came from the depths of his heart such petitions for me as I had never heard before. I rose from my knees to know what real prayer was."

THE PLACE OF PRAYER

Of everything we talk about, teach about, or even preach about in the Christian life — Nothing is discussed more and practiced less than prayer. Why do we struggle so much to pray? That question has many answers, and we've probably heard most of them, i.e., We're distracted, we're lazy, we're busy, we've had poor models, we lack a clear plan for how and when to pray, we're overwhelmed by the sheer volume of people and things to pray for, our Adversary opposes our praying, and the list goes on and on. But I think a significant reason for many of us is that we don't understand how Prayer works — or more accurately, we don't understand how Prayer doesn't work. For example, we read promises in Scripture like:

MARK 11:24 (NKJV) "Therefore I say to you, whatever things you ask when you pray, believe that you receive them, and you will have them."

After reading such scriptures, we then pray and don't see answers to our prayers. We're left asking, what's the problem? And we conclude that either our faith is so pitifully small that God essentially ignores them, or that there must be so many inscrutable, complicating factors inhibiting our answers that we end up as prayer cynics. Either way, the net effect is we're discouraged from praying much, unless we feel very desperate. Too often when we pray, we do as the song says, "Have a little talk with Jesus and tell Him all about our troubles." Then once we are done telling Him about our troubles we then get up and go on our way. Beloved, that is not real prayer. That makes prayer a one-directional and all about me. If we approach prayer in such a manner, it is nothing more than a means to get what we want. Like a spoiled child, we think that if we kick and scream enough, God will give in and magically produce the treats of life. Prayer is so much more than that. So, then what is prayer? I'm glad you asked. Therefore, allow me time to discuss that. Prayer, at a very shallow level, is asking for things that will better our own lives, here and now. However, prayer is much more than that. Prayer is spiritual communication between man and God, a two-way relationship in which man should not only talk to God but also listen to Him. Prayer is God's activity in our lives. Yet it is also our decided turning to God.

ROMANS 8:26 (NLT) "And the Holy Spirit helps us in our weakness. For example, we don't know what God wants us to pray for. But the Holy Spirit prays for us with groanings that cannot be expressed in words."

ROMANS 8:26 (MSG) "Meanwhile, the moment we get tired in the waiting, God's Spirit is right alongside helping us along. If we don't know how or what to pray, it doesn't matter. He does our praying in and for us, making prayer out of our wordless sighs, our aching groans."

There are times when we don't know what to say when we pray or even what to pray about. Prayer reaches beyond our words or vocabulary. Prayer then becomes profound self-examination with carefully cultivated awareness, as well as spontaneous and "inexpressible groaning." Prayer may be oral or mental, occasional, or constant, ejaculatory, or formal. Prayer can use written words, or your own words.

The Bible describes prayer as:

- "beseeching the Lord" (Exodus 32:11);
- "pouring out the soul before the Lord" (1 Samuel 1:15);
- "praying and crying to heaven" (2 Chronicles 32:20);
- "seeking unto God and making supplication" (Job 8:5);
- "drawing near to God" (Psalms 73:28);
- "bowing the knees" (Ephesians 3:14).

Prayer to God is like a child's conversation with his father. It is natural for a child to ask his father for the things he needs.

THE PLACE OF PRAYER

Prayer is that window that has the capacity to be used for great insight and contact—to be the means by which wonderful ideas can be created and great needs in the world can be identified.

Prayer is the intercourse of the soul with God, not in contemplation or meditation, but in direct address to him. Prayer deepens our faith which helps us come to a greater understanding of God's purpose for our life.

Lawrence Lovasik states in "The Basic Book of Catholic Prayer: How to Pray and Why," prayer is "an active attitude of the soul" that involves "an eager longing for grace." Yes, more than words, prayer is an attitude.

Prayer is the way that we come to terms with our joys, wants, and desires. It is the way we answer our longing for communion and compassion, and the way we seek ultimate completion.

Prayer is not merely a way to get something. When used that way, you reduce Prayer to a one-dimensional, self-centered practice, and will surely be unfulfilled when your requests aren't answered in just the way you want.

Prayer is not a stride toward the finish line. It is not a competition or a race: "If I say the right words, I'll win the prize!" That's no way to pray!

Prayer is not your answer to God's exam or a bargaining device. Prayer is not a means of instant gratification. It is not a pill for all ailments.

May I submit to you that Prayer is a Place. Now for the remainder of this book, we will discuss the Place of Prayer.

CHAPTER 2
PLACE OF TRANSFORMATION

*"Prayer is not a way of getting what we want,
but the way to become what God wants us to be."*

Have you ever heard the cliché, "Prayer changes things?" I've found that to be true. I remember my grandmother saying, "If prayer don't change your situation, it will definitely change how you see your situation." In other words, Prayer is a Place of Transformation.

In this chapter, we will discuss how prayer becomes the place of transformation. To do that, we must first understand what transformation is.

According to the Merriam-Webster Dictionary, transformation is:

1. An act, process, or instance of transforming or being transformed.
2. False hair worn especially by a woman to replace or supplement natural hair.
3. The operation of changing (as by rotation or mapping) one configuration or expression into another in accordance with a mathematical rule, especially: a change of variables or coordinates in which a function of new variables or coordinates is substituted for each original variable or coordinate.

THE PLACE OF PRAYER

4. An operation that converts (as by insertion, deletion, or permutation) one grammatical string (such as a sentence) into another also: a formal statement of such an operation.
5. Genetic modification of a bacterium by incorporation of free DNA from another bacterial cell also: genetic modification of a cell by the uptake and incorporation of exogenous DNA.

Now, if we dive into these definitions, there are a few words that stand out to me, for instance: process, operation, change, and convert. What is the significance of those words or even the definitions? Simply put:

- Prayer becomes the process of transformation.
- Prayer in operation transforms.
- Prayer is a change agent.
- What God has in the heavenly realm, prayer converts it into reality for the earthly realm.

Prayer is the place of transformation. However, for there to be a transformation, there must first be an invitation and an introspection. Let's look:

Prayer is an Invitation

While I was teaching at Kingdom Restoration World Outreach Ministries in Oklahoma City, OK, I felt led to ask the congregation, "If God is Sovereign, Omniscient, and Omni-present, then why do we have to pray?"

There were many responses, for instance: "God wants to hear what's in our heart," "To build our faith," "To show God we trust Him," "...because it's what we're supposed to do," "It's what we were taught," and more responses.

PLACE OF TRANSFORMATION

I then thanked them for their responses but challenged them to think deeper. I then heard God say, "Prayer is a means that invites me into your situation."

I was awed, then revelation started flowing, and this is where I went:

GENESIS 1:26 (NKJV) "Then God said, 'Let Us make man in Our image, according to Our likeness; let them have dominion over the fish of the sea, over the birds of the air, and over the cattle, over all the earth and over every creeping thing that creeps on the earth."

GENESIS 1:26 (NLT) "Then God said, 'Let us make human beings in our image, to be like ourselves. They will reign over the fish in the sea, the birds in the sky, the livestock, all the wild animals on the earth, and the small animals that scurry along the ground.'"

GENESIS 1:26 (MSG) "God spoke: 'Let us make human beings in our image, make them reflecting our nature so they can be responsible for the fish in the sea, the birds in the air, the cattle, and, yes, Earth itself, and every animal that moves on the face of Earth."

This verse is like a lease agreement. While the earth belongs to Me (God), I have given you "Dominion" according to the King James Version, "Reign over" according to the New Living Translation, and "Responsibility" according to the Message Bible.

At that moment, things were in our hands, and it was illegal for God and any other spirit to interfere in earth's affairs unless we invite them in.

If that scripture is not enough, then check this scripture out.

PSALM 115:16 (NKJV) "The heaven, even the heavens, are the LORD'S; but the earth He has given to the children of men."

PSALM 115:16 (NLT) "The heavens belong to the LORD, but he has given the earth to all humanity."

THE PLACE OF PRAYER

PSALM 115:16 (MSG) "The heaven of heavens is for God, but he put us in charge of the earth."

This is also why Jesus needed a body and came through Mary. Mary's womb was the incubator for Jesus' earthly legal body. Mary's birth canal provided the legal entryway for Jesus' earthly legal body into this earth realm.

Therefore, it is illegal for spirits, good or evil, to manifest or interfere with you and me unless we invite them in and/or agree with them.

Through prayer, we build an intimate relationship with God. Not only that, but prayer is an invitation to God for your situation. I can also it like this.

> **PRAYER IS A WAY TO INVITE GOD INTO YOUR WORLD.**

You may have gone to social media, made phone calls, texted, tweeted, and whatever else, and wondered why people are in your situation; well, you've invited them. Therefore, quit inviting people in and invite God in!

JEREMIAH 33:2-3 (NKJV) "Thus says the LORD who made it, the LORD who formed it to establish it (the LORD is His name): Call to Me, and I will answer you, and show you great and mighty things, which you do not know."

JEREMIAH 33:2-3 (NLT) "This is what the LORD says—the LORD who made the earth, who formed and established it, whose name is the LORD: Ask me and I will tell you remarkable secrets you do not know about things to come."

PLACE OF TRANSFORMATION

JEREMIAH 33:2-3 (MSG) "This is GOD's Message, the God who made earth, made it livable and lasting, known everywhere as GOD: 3 Call to me and I will answer you. I'll tell you marvelous and wondrous things that you could never figure out on your own."

Jeremiah desperately needed an intervention from the LORD. He was in prison for preaching the Word of God. At the same time, the citizens of Jerusalem were also suffering. The Babylonian army had already conquered the entire nation except for the capital Jerusalem. After being surrounded by them for eighteen months, food and water supplies were depleted. People were starving and dying of thirst, and the Babylonian army was ready to assault and capture the city. No doubt Jeremiah felt the pain of his people's sufferings as well as the anguish of his own imprisonment during those days of crisis.

Jeremiah then invited the LORD into this situation through prayer. God assured Jeremiah that He had the power to answer prayer. After all, He is the Creator, the very One who formed the universe and set it in place. The creator of the universe naturally has the power to answer prayer. God assured His prophet that He would answer his prayer by showing him His program for the future. God revealed His plans for His people by telling Jeremiah the wonderful things He had in store for them. God accepted the invitation through prayer.

PRAYER IS AN INVITATION.

Prayer Is Introspection

Prayer is our opportunity to move beyond our limitations. According to Rabbi Irwin Katsof's book "How to Get Your Prayers Answered," the Hebrew word for prayer, "li-heet-pallel," comes from the root "pallel," which means to inspect or examine. The prefix "li-heet" is the reflexive form - denoting an action that one does to

THE PLACE OF PRAYER

oneself. Li-heet-pallel, therefore, is an act of personal introspection. When we pray, we look inside and ask, "What do I need to change about myself in order to get what I really want out of life?"

This process of self-transformation means that today I may no longer be the same person who God said "No" to yesterday. Prayer is self-inspection, self-examination. It is through prayer that we learn about ourselves at deeper levels. We also come closer to God because we begin to understand how God can change us, not how we can change God.

Through the self-inspection conducted in prayer, we should be honest, open, and sincere with ourselves. We tap into the divine expression in side of us, gathering energy and finding aptitudes to which we might not normally gain access. Prayer is stepping away from the hustle and bustle of distractions. In this quiet place, we can see where we are weak and where we are strong. We can understand our role in the world. This leads to the next definition of prayer, which involves change. In order to change, we must examine ourselves.

PRAYER WILL CAUSE YOU TO CHECK YOUR MOTIVES.

JAMES 4:1-3 (NKJV) "Where do wars and fights come from among you? Do they not come from your desires for pleasure that war in your members? You lust and do not have. You murder and covet and cannot obtain. You fight and war. Yet you do not have because you do not ask. You ask and do not receive, because you ask amiss, that you may spend it on your pleasures."

JAMES 4:1-3 (NLT) "What is causing the quarrels and fights among you? Don't they come from the evil desires at war within you? You want what you don't have, so you scheme and kill to get it. You are jealous of what others have, but you can't get it, so you fight and wage war to take it away from them. Yet you don't have what you want because you don't ask God for it. And even when you ask, you don't get it because your motives are all wrong—you want only what will give you pleasure."

JAMES 4:1-3 (MSG) "Where do you think all these appalling wars and quarrels come from? Do you think they just happen? Think again. They come about because you want your own way, and fight for it deep inside yourselves. You lust for what you don't have and are willing to kill to get it. You want what isn't yours and will risk violence to get your hands on it. You wouldn't think of just asking God for it, would you? And why not? Because you know you'd be asking for what you have no right to. You're spoiled children, each wanting your own way."

There are two words translated "amiss" in the New Testament, Greek word "atopos," referring to that which is improper, harmful, or out of place, while Greek word "kakos," refers to that which is evil in the sense of a disaster, then to that which is wicked, morally wrong. This latter is the use of it in James 4:3. When we pray improperly, wishing harm or out of place, and by the same token, praying prayers that are sick, evil, morally wrong; these prayers are therefore amiss and cannot be granted by God. However, remember the enemy is also listening in. Therefore, when you pray such prayers, you are actually speaking curses.

While you want what you want and while you have the right to pray for what you want; Prayer, true prayer will cause you to be introspective.

The Path to Transformation

While we have cautioned ourselves against using prayer solely as a means to concentrate on the self, it is healthy to use the insight gained in prayer to transform ourselves for the better.

THE PLACE OF PRAYER

Through prayer, we cultivate a greater eye for the good and the bad, the healthy and the unhealthy. We see things for what they are and attain the bigger picture of what's truly important. As a result, prayer spurs us on to personal change. When we really get into the place of transformation, we will begin to pray as Jesus did in:

LUKE 22:42 (KJV) "Saying, Father, if thou be willing, remove this cup from me: nevertheless not my will, but thine, be done."

Therefore, through prayer, we should become God-centered, not self-centered. It is at this point that transformation takes place. All of a sudden, the material world is less important; the happiness afforded by financial wealth, worldly status, and the like, proves to be quite unfulfilling. Prayer, again, is a place of transformation. Therefore, praying in that vein says as one writer said:

> **PRAYER IS NOT A WAY OF GETTING WHAT WE WANT, BUT THE WAY TO BECOME WHAT GOD WANTS US TO BE**

CHAPTER 3
PLACE OF SUBMISSION

"Prayer is not a device for getting our wills done through heaven, but a desire that God's will may be done in earth through us."

~Author Unknown

MATTHEW 26:36-39 (NKJV) Then Jesus came with them to a place called Gethsemane, and said to the disciples, "Sit here while I go and pray over there." And He took with Him Peter and the two sons of Zebedee, and He began to be sorrowful and deeply distressed. Then He said to them, "My soul is exceedingly sorrowful, even to death. Stay here and watch with Me." He went a little farther and fell on His face, and prayed, saying, "O My Father, if it is possible, let this cup pass from Me; nevertheless, not as I will, but as You will."

In this passage, Christ demonstrates how prayer was a **place of submission** for Him. While knowing that death was imminent, Jesus, the man, was struggling with His Own Will and the Will of God, the Father. As believers, we often face similar struggles between our own desires and God's will.

THE PLACE OF PRAYER

Most of us know what we want and how we want it, often justifying our desires to ourselves and others. Yet, deep down, we sense the agony and internal conflict caused by pursuing our own will instead of God's. This leads to a fundamental question:

> **WHAT DO YOU DO WHEN WHAT YOU WANT IS NOT WHAT GOD WANTS FOR YOU?**

Jesus, the man, provides the answer. He withdrew alone to pray, not once, but three times, showing that aligning our will with God's may require persistent effort. He demonstrated that submission to God's will may not happen overnight but requires continued prayer and surrender until our will is in harmony with God's.

In essence, Jesus, the man, prayed until He could submit to the Will of the Father. He disappointed and disowned His Own Will, demonstrating the essence of submission.

Submit, in Hebrew, is kāhash, meaning to disappoint, fail, cringe, or disown. In Greek, it is hypotassō, meaning to obey or come under. Jesus obeyed the Father's will because He was under an assignment, showing that prayer is not about getting what we want from God but desiring God's will to be done through us on earth.

Praying in Faith

To enter the **Place of Submission**, we must pray in faith, which involves praying with assurance and acceptance. These two types of prayer are suited for different situations, and understanding how to use them is essential.

PLACE OF SUBMISSION

Praying with Assurance

This is a Faith–filled Prayer if there ever was one. Even though we may not know exactly what to do, nor know exactly how things are going to turn out; however, we do know that God is with us. Therefore, we believe that everything is going to work in our favor. This, beloved, is what we call praying with assurance.

For example, Elijah was a man just like us. He prayed earnestly that it would not rain, and it did not rain on the land for three and a half years. It was a time of great idolatry, as people were worshiping Baal, and Elijah prayed that it would not rain. You can read the story in 1 Kings 17-18. He must have been sure that what he prayed would happen because 1 Kings tells us Elijah went into the court of the tyrant, King Ahab, and said, "As the Lord, the God of Israel, lives, whom I serve, there will be neither dew nor rain in the next few years except at my word" (1 Kings 17:1).

You must be quite sure of the answer to your prayer to speak like that to the king. Elijah knew that what he prayed would happen. We know by observing what happened three and a half years later: After a long time, in the third year, the word of the Lord came to Elijah: "Go and present yourself to Ahab and I will send rain on the land" (1 Kings 18:1). God says to Elijah, "There will be rain." On the basis of that promise, Elijah speaks to Ahab and then begins to pray. God revealed what he was going to do, so when Elijah prayed, he had great confidence that what he prayed would happen. That's how it happened when the rains returned, and I think it is reasonable to assume that it happened the same way three years earlier when the rains stopped. God told Elijah what would happen, and so Elijah prayed with great assurance (1 Kings 18:42).

Beloved, Elijah showed us what Jesus said in the book of Mark:

THE PLACE OF PRAYER

MARK 11:24 (NKJV) "Therefore I say to you, whatever things you ask when you pray, believe that you receive them, and you will have them."

MARK 11:24 (NASB) "Therefore I say to you, all things for which you pray and ask, believe that you have received them, and they will be granted you."

MARK 11:24 (NLT) "I tell you, you can pray for anything, and if you believe that you've received it, it will be yours."

Now just as Elijah showed us what Jesus said in Mark 11:24, that's how it is with us. Or shall I say that's how we are to pray. Mark 11:24 is the epitome of what Praying with Assurance is. When you pray, believe what you prayed is already yours and Jesus said, "It will be yours."

Praying with Acceptance

World-renowned Gospel artist, also known as the "Queen of the Hammond B3," Albertina "Twinkie" Clark along with Bishop Richard "Mr. Clean" White; wrote and sang a song entitled, "Accept What God Allows." This song is exactly what Praying with Acceptance is all about.

Dictionary.com gives the following definition for Acceptance:

1. The act of taking or receiving something offered.
2. Reception; approval; favor.
3. The act of assenting or believing.
4. The fact or state of being accepted or acceptable.
5. An engagement to pay an order, draft, or bill of exchange when it becomes due, as by the person on whom it is drawn.
6. An order, draft, etc., that a person or bank has accepted as calling for payment and has thus promised to pay.

Of the above-mentioned definitions, the second definition of "reception; approval; favor" really hits home to me concerning prayer. Now with this particular definition of Acceptance, can we look at praying with acceptance in the following light:

Most people pray and expect God to give us instant gratification. We must realize that every prayer is answered, technically, with a "Yes, No, or Not Yet." It is the "No" and "Not Yet" that people consider a prayer that was not answered. However, in reality, the prayer was answered just not the way we wanted. This is when we Pray with Acceptance.

In the definition of Acceptance, there is "approval." When we are praying with acceptance, we are praying with this in mind, "God, I approve of how you answer this prayer." Let's be frank, most of us may not actually "like" nor "approve" what we encounter in life. However, approval is a way of praying with submission. When we pray, we don't know the outcome for sure, therefore, we pray with submission.

We dealt with Submit earlier; however, let's look a little deeper into Submission. The Greek word for submission is (hupotasso), which is a military term and it means "to subordinate…put under…"submit" or "subject" – You are actively choosing to put yourself under the authority, leadership, protection, and influence of another. This is not forced.

The extraordinary thing is the Prayer of Acceptance and the Prayer of Assurance are remarkably effective. It is not that these two kinds of prayers are greater and lesser. It is certainly not that one involves faith, and the other does not.

These two kinds of prayers are given to us for different situations. Let me give you an example of this second kind of praying: A man with leprosy came to him and begged him on his knees, "If you are willing, you can make me clean" (Mark 1:40). From the man's prayer,

THE PLACE OF PRAYER

it is clear that he knows Christ can heal him: "You can make me clean." There is no doubt there. However, what he does not know is if it is Christ's purpose to make him clean: "If you are willing…" He does not know what the outcome will be. To ask with assurance would be presumption. Therefore, he asked with "Acceptance," and in this way, he honors Christ. Then we read, "Filled with compassion, Jesus reached out his hand and touched the man. 'I am willing,' he said. 'Be clean!'" (Mark 1:41). This is not an inferior kind of praying. We pray with assurance when God has made the outcome clear, and with acceptance when the outcome is unknown.

To surmise the Place of Submission, we must know that with God the outcome is known and unknown. It's unknown because we may not know exactly what is going to happen or how it will happen, but known because we know God has everything under control. Therefore,

> **WE PRAY, NOT IN THE KNOWING OF THE OUTCOME, BUT IN SUBMISSION TO THE OUTCOME.**

Now before we close this chapter, I feel I must tell you the other word that stood out to me in the definition of acceptance; "Favor." You may be wondering what does "Favor" have to do with prayer? I'm glad you were, so let me explain.

It blessed me when I saw "Favor" as part of the definition of acceptance. Or as the church would say, "My soul got happy" when I saw that. It is in Praying with Acceptance, being submitted to the outcome that becomes a door or a pathway to favor. When we pray that way, we are saying, "God, I trust You!" That is when God says in return, "Since you trust Me, I'll favor you!" That sent me into a praise.

PLACE OF SUBMISSION

To know that even though the answer to what I prayed for may not be what I expected, liked, or wanted; I trusted God. We must understand that the answers to our prayers are God working for my good. This is how it came to my spirit:

> **When I trust God, he favors me!**

CHAPTER 4
PLACE OF PREPARATION

Prayer will prepare you for what's ahead.

MATTHEW 26:45-46 (NKJV) Then He came to His disciples and said to them, "Are you still sleeping and resting? Behold, the hour is at hand, and the Son of Man is being betrayed into the hands of sinners. Rise, let us be going. See, My betrayer is at hand.

Merriam–Webster defines "preparation" as "the action or process of making something ready for use or service or of getting ready for some occasion, test, or duty."

Taking this definition of preparation; Prayer then becomes part of our strategy that makes us ready for what is to come. Prayer is one of the things God uses in consideration for your promotion. Prayer is also what makes us ready to be used of God.

Many people misinterpret what it means to be used by God. They mistakenly think it has to do with prophesying, preaching, singing, etc. You know, those performances. However, being used by God are those tough moments, moments when you feel like giving up and throwing in the towel. Being used by God are those moments of betrayal, being lied on and misunderstood; yet all for His Glory.

THE PLACE OF PRAYER

As a matter of fact, a great example of being used by God is Jesus Christ, especially what He endured for mankind when He laid His life down to die on the cross. Therefore, not only did prayer prepare Jesus for His imminent death of the cross, but Prayer also prepared Jesus for being betrayed by Judas.

Prayer will prepare you for what lies ahead. In the Garden of Gethsemane when Jesus asked God to remove the bitter cup, God did not give Jesus what He asked; that is, God did not remove the cup. Jesus had to drink the cup, but God did answer His prayer. God relieved the agony and strengthened Him to bear the cup. God kept Him from failing. God sometimes answers our prayers with "No." However, He strengthens us and gives us what we need to sustain us. However, in those moments, most of us may not recognize what God is doing nor realize how much we needed it.

Prayer prepares you by strengthening you for the task at hand. Even when you feel like you are in it by yourself, God has a way of letting you know that you are not. For instance, just like He did Jesus, God sent Angels to strengthen and encourage Jesus, He will do the same for you and I.

Do you recall Matthew chapter 4 right after Jesus had fasted and prayed 40 days and 40 nights? Jesus was hungry. Now I know the bible says He fasted but didn't mention that He prayed. However, we know that fasting and prayer go together. Fasting without prayer is just a diet. Not to mention to fast that long you better pray.

Anyhow, after He fasted 40 days and nights, the devil came to tempt Jesus. First, Satan tried to tempt Jesus by coming after His Will saying, "I know you are hungry, turn this bread into stone." Jesus responds to the Devil with the Word by quoting Deuteronomy, saying, "Man shall not live by bread alone, but by every word that proceeds from the mouth of God."

That wasn't enough. Satan then tries to tempt Jesus a second time by coming after His Power. He took Jesus to the Holy City, took Him to the pinnacle of the temple and then said, "Since you are the Son of God, jump."

The Devil attempted to sway Jesus by quoting Psalm 91, suggesting that angels would protect Him from harm. Jesus countered with a reminder from Deuteronomy, cautioning against testing God. Undeterred, Satan made a final bid for Jesus' allegiance by promising earthly kingdoms in exchange for worship. Jesus swiftly rebuked Satan, affirming allegiance to God alone. With the test concluded, angels ministered to Jesus, highlighting the power of His prayer during fasting.

At Kingdom Life Church, I often emphasize to my congregation that while prayer may not alter circumstances as desired, it fosters personal transformation amid adversity. Prayer, in essence, alters our perspective on life's challenges.

What exactly is perspective? Merriam–Webster Dictionary defines it as the ability to perceive things in their true context or significance. Through prayer, our perception gains depth, enabling us to grasp the truth and prioritize effectively.

Consider this: your perspective shapes your outlook, which in turn influences your outcome. Therefore, prayer not only prepares us for the future but also grants us revelation, illuminating the significance of our experiences.

Ultimately, prayer equips us to navigate life's twists and turns with clarity and resolve, unveiling the deeper truths behind every situation. As we embrace this perspective, we understand that true preparation yields profound insights.

WITH PREPARATION COMES REVELATION.

CHAPTER 5
PLACE OF REVELATION

"Revelations during prayer will last a lifetime."

In our previous discussion on perspective, we explored how prayer can transform our view of circumstances. We adopted Merriam-Webster's definition of perspective as "the capacity to view things in their true relations or relative importance." Now, let's delve deeper into this concept.

When our perspective shifts through prayer, it enables us to handle what we see with greater depth and clarity. We begin to perceive the truth of situations and discern what truly matters. This shift in perspective lays the groundwork for revelations during prayer.

Consider Jesus in the Garden of Gethsemane. While He already knew who His betrayer was, prayer prepared Him to recognize the precise moment when His betrayer and captors arrived to apprehend Him. Without this revelation during prayer, Jesus may not have been able to alert His disciples.

According to Merriam-Webster, revelation is "an act of revealing or communicating divine truth" or "something that is revealed by God to humans." In simple terms, prayer serves as the conduit through which God communicates His divine truth and enlightens our understanding.

THE PLACE OF PRAYER

Prayer brings understanding. Despite common misconceptions, questioning God is not inherently sinful. In fact, the Bible grants us permission to seek understanding. As it says:

MATTHEW 7:7-8 (NKJV) "Ask, and it will be given to you; seek, and you will find; knock, and it will be opened to you. For everyone who asks receives, and he who seeks finds, and to him who knocks it will be opened."

MATTHEW 7:7-8 (NLT) "Keep on asking, and you will receive what you ask for. Keep on seeking, and you will find. Keep on knocking, and the door will be opened to you. For everyone who asks, receives. Everyone who seeks, finds. And to everyone who knocks, the door will be opened."

MATTHEW 7:7-8 (MSG) "Don't bargain with God. Be direct. Ask for what you need. This isn't a cat-and-mouse, hide-and-seek game we're in."

Many don't understand that you can ask God questions and you should especially if you need clarity or understanding. Since many don't have that understanding, they do as the Message Bible Version says, they try to "bargain with God." Prayer is not a place to bargain, but rather a place to get results. There have been many times or even situations in my life where I simply didn't understand what was going on, why it was happening or how it could be happening. I had to go to God for understanding. I needed revelation.

Jesus said to "Ask, and it will be given to you;" that sounds like permission to question God. As a matter of fact, Jesus asked God a question while on the cross. Even though He spoke of His own death not many days before; He still belted out according to Matthew 27:46, "Eli, Eli, lama sabachthani?" that is, "My God, My God, why have You forsaken Me?" Jesus shows us that in order to get some understanding or get the answers, we must ask.

PLACE OF REVELATION

During this time in the life of Christ, we gain a lot of revelation about Christ through His last words. We know them now as the Seven Last Sayings of Christ. The traditional order of the sayings are found accordingly:

> Luke 23:34: Father, forgive them, for they know not what they do.
>
> Luke 23:43: Verily, I say unto you today, thou shalt be with me in paradise.
>
> John 19:26–27: Woman, behold thy son. (Says to disciple) Behold thy mother.
>
> Matthew 27:46 and Mark 15:34: My God, My God, why have you forsaken me?
>
> John 19:28: I thirst.
>
> John 19:30: It is finished.
>
> Luke 23:46: Father, into thy hands I commit my spirit.
>
> According to The International Standard Bible Encyclopedia by Geoffrey W. Bromiley 1988 p. 426, these seven sayings are called words of:
>
> 1. Forgiveness
> 2. Salvation
> 3. Relationship
> 4. Abandonment
> 5. Distress
> 6. Triumph
> 7. Reunion

However, these statements are of tremendous significance because they reveal that Jesus was consistent in His life and in His message until the end. Let's look deeper:

> 1. "Father, forgive them, for they know not what they do" (Luke 23:34). This first of seven sayings of Jesus shows that He was thinking of others until the end of His life.

THE PLACE OF PRAYER

2. "Today you will be with me in Paradise" (Luke 23:43). Not only did Jesus forgive those who crucified Him, He also forgave one of the thieves crucified next to Him.
3. "Woman, behold your Son" (John 19:26).
4. "My God, my God, why have you forsaken me?" (Matthew 27:46). The third and fourth statements reveal the humanity of Christ. The fourth saying of Jesus from the cross is probably the most difficult for us to understand. The sinless Son of God who had been, from all eternity, in an intimate relationship with His Father, is now spiritually separated from Him. When the sins of the world were put upon Jesus there was, for the first time, a separation between the Father and the Son.

The Bible records something happened between them that we can only understand through the eye of faith. That is, that God was in Christ reconciling the world to himself (2 Cor 5:19). The Father was placing the sins of the world upon the Son in order that everything in the universe that had been affected by sin could again be made right with God. Jesus was suffering the pain and separation that we deserve: "For he made him who knew no sin to be sin for us, that we might become the righteousness of God in him" (2 Cor 5:21).

In order for this to occur, the Father had to forsake the Son and punish Him on our behalf.

5. "I thirst" (John 19:28). The fifth statement that Jesus made from the cross reminds us again that He suffered as a human being.
6. "It is finished" (John 19:30). The sixth statement from Jesus while on the cross was a cry of victory. It showed Jesus was a finisher. Jesus finished the job that the Father gave him to do.
7. "Father, into your hands I commend my spirit" (Luke 23:46). In this final statement, it reveals that Jesus trusted the Father.

Prayer Reveals

While prayer shifts our perspective, gives clarity, and understanding, but what does prayer really reveal? Too many want God to reveal things, change things, and even people when they pray, however most of the same people are not willing to allow God to reveal or change them. Prayer has a way of revealing Christ to us and His desires for us.

However, that's not the only thing prayer reveals. In reality, prayer reveals your perspective or how you see things. Prayer reveals your motives or your reasons for that prayer. Prayer reveals your intentions or what you are really targeting in prayer. Prayer also reveals your desires or your longings. Prayer will reveal what's really in your heart. Ultimately, prayer reveals the real you.

If you have a real prayer journal or if you really keep track of your prayers, go back over them, and actually pay attention to the things you pray. Assuming you are being real, honest, and going for broke in prayer, it will reveal your true feelings, emotions and even thoughts. You can find out more about yourself in real true prayer than you can in almost anything else.

For instance, you begin to pray for someone, and here is your prayer:

"Dear heavenly Father, I adore you and I love you. Lord, you know I wanted that business deal to go through for me. God, I don't understand how a person can play people like that and then steal their ideas. God, I know you have a special place in hell for a person like that. Lord, I ask you get them. You know I've been faithful to You, and they treated me like that. Your Word says, Vengeances is Mine, so God get them. I declare whatever they are trying to accomplish, it will fail and fall. In Jesus Name I pray, Amen!"

THE PLACE OF PRAYER

How often have we prayed a prayer similar to that? You may not see anything wrong with that prayer, however, if you really dissect it, you will find a lot wrong with it. When you really want to know what is being revealed, you must answer some tough questions like: Why did I pray this? Your answer, they got over on my in a business deal. So, I want God to make their thing fall. How did them getting over me make me feel? Your answer, hurt and angry. As a result, I want God to get them.

So, in that prayer what was revealed? That prayer revealed, you prayed out of the motive of hurt and angry therefore, your intent was really revenge. It also revealed that your desire was to succeed in that business deal. What is also missed is that this really wasn't a prayer, it was a word curse and even witchcraft and we didn't even know it.

Again, Prayer is a place of Revelation. We have just seen what prayer is really revealing. I'm at a place now where I can see more on my knees than my education has shown me on my tiptoes. That has caused me to realize:

THINGS THAT BEGIN IN PRAYER USUALLY END WITH REVELATION!

CHAPTER 6
A PLACE OF DECISION

"If a care is too small to be made into a prayer, then it can only become a temporary win and not a lasting victory."

~Dr. Samuel D. Abbott

MATTHEW 26:39 (NKJV) He went a little farther and fell on His face, and prayed, saying, "O My Father, if it is possible, let this cup pass from Me; nevertheless, not as I will, but as You will."

Merriam–Webster defines "decision" as:

- The act or process of deciding
- A determination arrived at after consideration
- A report of a conclusion
- A determination
- A Win specifically, combat sports: a victory based on points awarded

Based on these definitions of decision, there are a few ways pertaining to prayer we can go. However, I first want you to know that Jesus showed us, on more than one occasion, prayer is the first part of the process to the Cross.

THE PLACE OF PRAYER

With the Cross in the backdrop of Jesus' immediate future, He was weighted with the choice to follow through with the plan or have a change of mind and do something different. Jesus had a decision to make. So, what did He do? He prayed.

While Jesus was in the Garden of Gethsemane, He said, "O My Father, if it is possible, let this cup pass from Me. . ." This statement in prayer, Jesus simply asked God to take the death of the Cross away. However, let's look at His next statement, ". . . nevertheless, not as I will, but as You will." It is this statement in the same prayer that shows that Jesus decided to submit to the death of the Cross. It is also this statement that showed Jesus was determined to do the Will of God the Father.

These statements reiterate what has already been discussed earlier in this book, prayer was the place that Jesus submitted to the death of Cross. Prayer also prepared him for death of the Cross, it was also in Prayer that Jesus decided to submit. Finally, prayer revealed His betrayer had come.

MATTHEW 26:46–53 (NKJV) Rise, let us be going. See, My betrayer is at hand." And while He was still speaking, behold, Judas, one of the twelve, with a great multitude with swords and clubs, came from the chief priests and elders of the people. Now His betrayer had given them a sign, saying, "Whomever I kiss, He is the One; seize Him." Immediately he went up to Jesus and said, "Greetings, Rabbi!" and kissed Him. But Jesus said to him, "Friend, why have you come?" Then they came and laid hands-on Jesus and took Him. And suddenly, one of those who were with Jesus stretched out his hand and drew his sword, struck the servant of the high priest, and cut off his ear. But Jesus said to him, "Put your sword in its place, for all who take the sword will perish by the sword. Or do you think that I cannot now pray to My Father, and He will provide Me with more than twelve legions of angels?

A PLACE OF DECISION

Just like the above example, prayer was the place that Jesus submitted to the process of death of Cross. Which means He had to submit to being captured by His betrayer and his crew. Because Jesus prayed, He was also prepared for what was to come. Therefore, Jesus decided to go with his Betrayer and his people. Rememberin verse 53, Jesus said, He could pray, and God would send more than twelve legions of angels to fight for Him. However, Jesus decided to go. Jesus showed us that we should not make a decision without prayer. Prayer should be our first resort not our last.

Our Decision

How many times have you had to make a decision about something? Did you pray about it or did you just make a decision based on feeling, data, or others' suggestions? We've all been there at some point in our lives. The Bible tells us:

PROVERBS 3:5 "In all your ways acknowledge Him and He shall direct your paths."

Why is this point so important? Let me explain it by highlighting another meaning of decision, "A Win specifically, combat sports: a victory based on points awarded."

Considering this definition, prayer then becomes the way we win. It is in prayer where we become victorious; therefore, our place of decision becomes the place where we win.

There have been times in my life where I have had the upper hand, the goods on someone, or even the advantage. For instance, there have been people who opposed me, lied on me, and even tried to undermine me. I had the information and proof that could have really damaged them and their reputation and made me the winner, so to speak. However, in prayer, God reminded me that isn't the victory I should want (it's definitely not what He wanted). He reminded me the greatest victory I could get is winning them over to Christ. How was that to happen? They knew I had the goods on them, so to speak, but the fact that I didn't use it to come out on top showed them Christ-like character. It wasn't long before they apologized and gave their life to Christ. Prayer gave me and them, for that matter, real victory.

Prayer, being a place of revelation, will reveal that even though you have what seems to be an advantage, it really isn't. Prayer will reveal that your decision or your pre-determined outcome is simply not God's Will. Prayer will ultimately remind you that your decision could be a temporary win, yet not the outcome nor lasting or ultimate victory God has for you.

Beloved, Jesus showed us prayer was the place of victory for Him. At any time, He could have called more than twelve legions of angels down and conquered his betrayer and his crew; however, that wasn't the victory God had in mind. Jesus said,

MATTHEW 26:56 (NKJV) "But all this was done that the Scriptures of the prophets might be fulfilled." Then all the disciples forsook Him and fled."

What Jesus ultimately showed us was, "why take this temporary win when victory over death, hell, and the grave are still waiting, not to mention victory for countless others through eternal life?"

Future

Prayer, the place of decision, shapes your future. Your victory and your future are predicated on your place of decision. I must also tell you that there are times when victory for others is tied to your place of decision.

Do you realize that a child of God in prayer affects decisions in heaven? Most people don't realize that their decisions on earth can and do govern movements in heaven. The Lord declared:

A PLACE OF DECISION

MATTHEW 18:18 (NKJV) "Assuredly, I say to you, whatever you bind on earth will be bound in heaven, and whatever you loose on earth will be loosed in heaven.

Let me explain it this way: whatever you ask and or agree with in prayer, the decision is made in heaven to stand with you. Conversely, whatever you stand firm against in prayer, the decision is made in heaven to back you and stand firm against it as well. In short, whatever you allow, God will allow, and whatever you disallow, God will disallow.

However, I feel we must go a little deeper with the thought of your prayers affecting the decisions in heaven. There are some decisions, even in heaven, that can be changed because of prayer being the place of decisions. To investigate this provocative thought, let's look in the Bible at:

EXODUS 32:9–14 (KJV) And the LORD said unto Moses, I have seen this people, and, behold, it is a stiffnecked people: Now therefore let me alone, that my wrath may wax hot against them, and that I may consume them: and I will make of thee a great nation. And Moses besought the LORD his God, and said, LORD, why doth thy wrath wax hot against thy people, which thou hast brought forth out of the land of Egypt with great power, and with a mighty hand? Wherefore should the Egyptians speak, and say, For mischief did he bring them out, to slay them in the mountains, and to consume them from the face of the earth? Turn from thy fierce wrath, and repent of this evil against thy people. Remember Abraham, Isaac, and Israel, thy servants, to whom thou swarest by thine own self, and saidst unto them, I will multiply your seed as the stars of heaven, and all this land that I have spoken of will I give unto your seed, and they shall inherit it forever. And the LORD repented of the evil which he thought to do unto his people.

THE PLACE OF PRAYER

In the background of this text, we find Moses coming down the mountain from receiving the Ten Commandments from God, after God has spent two chapters in an ongoing dialogue with Moses. Moses finds that he has been with God too long for the people who have been waiting.

While Moses has been in communion with God, the Children of Israel coerced Aaron to lead them. Then they began to collect their earrings, necklaces, and bracelets. They threw them into a furnace and began to design their golden calf to worship.

While Moses is still communing, talking, or praying to God, God, being omniscient, gets upset with the Children of Israel for making an idol to worship. He then sends Moses down the mountain to get his people. God tells Moses He was about to wipe the people out.

Moses did something amazing. God disowned the people and gave them to Moses, and Moses reminded God they were His people. He told God doing this would make Him look bad to the rest of the world. Not only that, but he reminded God of His promises to the people and to Moses. As a result, God repented or as the New Living Translation says, "God changed His mind."

EXODUS 32:14 (NLT) "So the LORD changed his mind about the terrible disaster he had threatened to bring on his people."

Moses was in constant communication with God. What is prayer? It is communication between man and God. Prayer is not all about you talking to God, but there are times when God talks to you. It is a dialogue. Through the conversation or prayers of Moses, God changed His mind, and instead of wiping the people out, He saved them. Prayer, the place of decision, can be the determining factor that alters the movements in heaven concerning the earth.

A PLACE OF DECISION

I tell Kingdom Life International, the church I pastor, all the time, "You are one decision away from being a millionaire or one decision away from life in prison. That decision is up to you."

Because we are the sum of all the decisions we make, prayer is absolutely essential. Your next decision could be your best decision. Your next decision can shift and shape the rest of your life. Your next decision must not only be a good decision, but it must be a God decision; therefore, prayer must be the place of decision.

CHAPTER 7
A PLACE OF SUPERNATURAL PROTECTION

Job tells us there is a secret place, known and available only to God's children. And when God's children enter it, only then is the power of God activated on their behalf and on behalf of those in desperate need:

JOB 28:7-8 (KJV) "There is a path which no fowl knoweth, and which the vulture's eye hath not seen: The lion's whelps have not trodden it, nor the fierce lion passed by it."

There is a path, a place which no fowl knows. That place is the secret place, that glorious place so secure and protected that no demonic power can find it. It is a place hidden in God that no vulture's eye has seen. No demon on earth nor Satan, the enemy of our souls, has seen or knows. It is a place of refuge, a place of safety that no lion's whelps (principalities and powers) pass by—not even the lion, Satan. That place is the place of Prayer.

THE PLACE OF PRAYER

PRAYER IS THE PLACE OF SUPERNATURAL

Psalm 91 does a good job of talking about that place of protection:

PSALM 91:1-7 (NKJV) He who dwells in the secret place of the Most High Shall abide under the shadow of the Almighty. I will say of the LORD, "He is my refuge and my fortress; My God, in Him I will trust." Surely He shall deliver you from the snare of the fowler And from the perilous pestilence. He shall cover you with His feathers, And under His wings you shall take refuge; His truth shall be your shield and buckler. You shall not be afraid of the terror by night, Nor of the arrow that flies by day, Nor of the pestilence that walks in darkness, Nor of the destruction that lays waste at noonday. A thousand may fall at your side, And ten thousand at your right hand; But it shall not come near you.

PSALM 91:1-7 (MSG) You who sit down in the High God's presence, spend the night in Shaddai's shadow, Say this: "GOD, you're my refuge. I trust in you and I'm safe!" That's right—he rescues you from hidden traps, shields you from deadly hazards. His huge outstretched arms protect you— under them you're perfectly safe; his arms fend off all harm. Fear nothing—not wild wolves in the night, not flying arrows in the day, Not disease that prowls through the darkness, not disaster that erupts at high noon. Even though others succumb all around, drop like flies right.

That place is the place of prayer. The psalmist in Psalm 91 tells us it is in that secret place that you will find the Lord to be your refuge and fortress, and it is in that secret place that He covers you with His wings so that no evil will befall you nor will any plague come nigh to your dwelling. That secret path, that secret place is prayer.

A PLACE OF SUPERNATURAL PROTECTION

Vocabulary.com defines protection as:

1. The activity of protecting someone or something
2. The condition of being protected
3. Shelter
4. A covering that is intended to protect from damage or injury

With these definitions in mind, let's look at Psalm 121:

PSALM 121:5–8 (NKJV) The LORD is your keeper; The LORD is your shade at your right hand. The sun shall not strike you by day, Nor the moon by night. The LORD shall preserve you from all evil; He shall preserve your soul. The LORD shall preserve your going out and your coming in From this time forth, and even forevermore.

PSALM 121:5–8 (NLT) The LORD himself watches over you! The LORD stands beside you as your protective shade. The sun will not harm you by day, nor the moon at night. The LORD keeps you from all harm and watches over your life. The LORD keeps watch over you as you come and go, both now and forever.

This Psalm is a prayer, and the definition of protection is spelled out in this Psalm. The Lord is your keeper, and He watches over you. He gives you shade, shelter, or covering from the sun. The Lord won't let nothing harm you. The definition of protection is spelled out in this Psalm. This is the Place of Prayer.

When there is demonic activity, prayer is that source of protection, whether it be physical, mental, emotional, spiritual, or even financial. Prayer forms a shield around us. It puts us under the favor of God, who is ultimately far more powerful than any "demonic" force.

Intercessory Prayer is a strong key to prayer being a shield or prayer the place of protection. For intercessors, as Pastor John F. Hannah, pastor of New Life Southeast in Chicago, IL says, "Intercessors are the

THE PLACE OF PRAYER

snipers in the spirit. They are like special forces in the military." Therefore, intercessors and intercessory prayers protect us from danger seen and danger unseen.

Think of the Roman phalanx, with all the soldiers lifting their individual shields to ensure protection over the whole company. In a similar way, when we pray, we are lifting our individual shields bringing protection over not just our lives, but over the ones we are praying for. Many also fail to realize, prayer will also strengthen the individual who prays against the vices and temptations within them. See Satan is the ultimate strategist. He studies us and finds our weaknesses and vices. Then he uses them against us.

Therefore, as we pray, we lift and interlock spiritual shields, bringing us protection from the attacks of the enemy, as well as releasing the favor of God over our lives. We must remember, without prayer we would be at the mercy of the enemy, therefore, it is imperative that we stay in that place of Prayer – being that it is the place of supernatural protection.

CHAPTER 8
A PLACE OF DIVINE ORCHESTRATION

DANIEL 10:1-12 (NKJV) "In the third year of Cyrus king of Persia a message was revealed to Daniel, whose name was called Belteshazzar. The message was true, but the appointed time was long; and he understood the message, and had understanding of the vision. In those days I, Daniel, was mourning three full weeks. I ate no pleasant food, no meat or wine came into my mouth, nor did I anoint myself at all, till three whole weeks were fulfilled. Now on the twenty-fourth day of the first month, as I was by the side of the great river, that is, the Tigris, I lifted my eyes and looked, and behold, a certain man clothed in linen, whose waist was girded with gold of Uphaz! His body was like beryl, his face like the appearance of lightning, his eyes like torches of fire, his arms and feet like burnished bronze in color, and the sound of his words like the voice of a multitude. And I, Daniel, alone saw the vision, for the men who were with me did not see the vision; but a great terror fell upon them, so that they fled to hide themselves. Therefore, I was left alone when I saw this great vision, and no strength remained in me; for my vigor was turned to frailty in me, and I retained no strength. Yet I heard the sound of his words; and while I heard the sound of his words I was in a deep sleep on my face, with my face to the ground. Suddenly, a hand touched me, which made me tremble on my knees and on the palms

THE PLACE OF PRAYER

of my hands. And he said to me, "O Daniel, man greatly beloved, understand the words that I speak to you, and stand upright, for I have now been sent to you." While he was speaking this word to me, I stood trembling. Then he said to me, "Do not fear, Daniel, for from the first day that you set your heart to understand, and to humble yourself before your God, your words were heard; and I have come because of your words."

> **SATAN MAY LAUGH AT YOU, MOCK YOU, AND EVEN RIDICULE YOU, HOWEVER, HE TREMBLES WHEN YOU PRAY.**

There are times when life is not fair, when people have come against us, when we're fighting an illness, or things around us seem to be going haywire; that's when you must know that God is still in control, and He wouldn't have allowed it if it wasn't going to work for your good. Therefore, when you pray, and it looks like things aren't moving; don't stop praying. Your prayers are orchestrating the heavens to act on your behalf. So don't get discouraged when you don't understand it. Know that God is up to something.

> **TRUE PRAYER IS THE ONE WEAPON THE ENEMY CANNOT DUPLICATE OR COUNTERFEIT.**

Cambridge Dictionary defines 'orchestration' as:

1. To plan and organize something carefully and sometimes secretly in order to achieve a desired result.

2. To organize something complicated in a very careful and sometimes secret way, especially in order to gain an advantage for oneself."

What is Divine Orchestration?

What an amazing truth—that the One who is the great conductor of the universe knows what you are facing right now. And He is extending His mercy and power towards you.

Think of the word "symphony." It comes from the Greek word sumphonos; which means "sounds brought together" or "voices brought together." For things to be 'symphonious' with each other, they must be in one accord with one another. They should complement each other, or they are harmonious in a pleasing way. In an instrumental or choral orchestration, different musicians play different notes on different instruments, or different voices sing different parts; however, because they do so in a carefully planned and intentional way, and under a single direction, the end result is unified and symphonious.

The Scripture says, "The steps of a good man are orchestrated by the Lord" (Psalm 37:23).

I know there are many scriptures that state in some form to not add not take away from the Word. However, in this case, may I change one word? If so, I would like to change "ordered" to "orchestrated." Therefore, the steps of a good man are orchestrated by the Lord. Nothing happens randomly, the promotion, the times you see favor, the closed doors, the disappointments, and the betrayals, because someone was and is praying for you or interceding on your behalf, their prayers began to orchestrate the heavens. God now uses those prayers as setups to move you up to a new level of your destiny.

THE PLACE OF PRAYER

Our prayers, especially corporately or in intercession; this is especially true when those sounds and voices are brought together in one accord, take us to the place of orchestration.

In the place of orchestration, God is working in the background, behind the scenes, in the unseen realm to bring about His purpose in your life as a response to your prayers. In other words, there is a place in prayer where God says, "Regardless of what it looks like right now, I am working within the scenes, and I am moving behind the scenes."

Friends, know that God is constantly working on your behalf, and no issue is beyond His reach. As a matter of fact, whatever the devil has been doing to you this year. Whatever he has attacked you with, don't worry about it, just pray, and watch your prayers orchestrate the heavens on your behalf.

When Daniel prayed, God released his answer but because the Prince of Persia held the answer up, Daniel's continued prayers caused God to orchestrate the heavens for Daniel's benefit. When you pray with persistence through faith, you enter a place where your prayers begin to move, ignite, and incite orchestration in heaven. The prince of Persia withheld the answer. As a matter of fact, the more Daniel prayed the more the prince had to withhold. However, because Daniel entered a place in prayer that moved God so that He sent Michael to handle the Prince of Persia and to release his answer.

Beloved, we must remember that sumphonos means "sounds brought together," therefore, in the Place of Prayer that causes orchestration, when our sound aligns with heaven's sound, God has no choice but to orchestrate things on our behalf and in our favor.

CHAPTER 9
A PLACE OF DELIVERANCE

Acts 16:16–26 (NKJV) Now it happened, as we went to prayer, that a certain slave girl possessed with a spirit of divination met us, who brought her masters much profit by fortune-telling. This girl followed Paul and us, and cried out, saying, "These men are the servants of the Most High God, who proclaim to us the way of salvation." And this she did for many days. But Paul, greatly annoyed, turned and said to the spirit, "I command you in the name of Jesus Christ to come out of her." And he came out that very hour. But when her masters saw that their hope of profit was gone, they seized Paul and Silas and dragged them into the marketplace to the authorities. And they brought them to the magistrates, and said, "These men, being Jews, exceedingly trouble our city; and they teach customs which are not lawful for us, being Romans, to receive or observe." Then the multitude rose up together against them; and the magistrates tore off their clothes and commanded them to be beaten with rods. And when they had laid many stripes on them, they threw them into prison, commanding the jailer to keep them securely. Having received such a charge, he put them into the inner prison and fastened their feet in the stocks. But at midnight Paul and Silas were praying and singing hymns to God, and the prisoners were listening to them. Suddenly there was a great earthquake, so that the foundations of the prison were shaken;

THE PLACE OF PRAYER

and immediately all the doors were opened, and everyone's chains were loosed.

In Acts 16, Paul and Silas are on their way to prayer when they encounter a detour of their own. The spirit inside the fortune-telling girl knew the truth about God's power, and she followed them for days saying the same thing over and over. Eventually, Paul cast the spirit out of her (v.18). Her masters were furious to lose their livelihood and took Paul and Silas to the chief magistrates, who threw them in prison. Now, Paul and Silas could choose to be angry and frustrated. They could feel bad for themselves or stress about the fact that their plans were thrown off track. They could keep to themselves and be rude to the other prisoners. But that's not what they did. Instead, they did what they were intending to do in the first place. They prayed and sang praises.

Acts 16:25 (NKJV) But at midnight Paul and Silas were praying and singing hymns to God, and the prisoners were listening to them.

In a frustrating situation, Paul and Silas's direct response to their situation was to pray and praise God. Prayer became a place of deliverance, and a midnight deliverance probably isn't what anyone expected. But the unexpected is often where God shows up and does the miraculous.

Webster's 1828 Dictionary Defines Deliverance as:

1. Release from captivity, slavery, oppression, or any restraint.
2. Rescue from danger or any evil.
3. The act of bringing forth children.
4. The act of giving or transferring from one to another.
5. The act of speaking or pronouncing; utterance.
6. Acquittal of a prisoner, by the verdict of a jury.

Cambridge Dictionary Defines Deliverance as: The state of being saved from a painful or bad experience.

A PLACE OF DELIVERANCE

Through those definitions, we can see that it was how Paul and Silas prayed. They entered a place of deliverance, and as a result, they ended up leading the jailor and an entire family to the Lord. It is vital that we continue to pray. We may not see what is going on, but as the last chapter stated, in prayer, we get in a place where God is orchestrating things behind the scenes; your prayers will cause your family members, friends, and other loved ones to be set free, rescued, released, acquitted – delivered.

There is also something that we are not going to overlook; that being Paul and Silas also sang praises. In the last chapter, we also discussed that orchestration is sumphonos which means, "sounds brought together." In this case, Paul and Silas brought two places together in one. They brought the place of orchestration and the place of deliverance together. Therefore, not only did they enter the place of deliverance in prayer, but they also sang praise, which takes us to the place of orchestration. When their sound aligned with heaven's sound, God had no choice but to cause an earthquake and the doors came open, bands were loosed, and people were saved.

All of this was possible because Paul and Silas were actually persistent in prayer. Remember they were on their way to pray when they got sidetracked by the woman who had the spirit of divination. Maybe you're like me—you don't like disruptions, distractions, or things that mess up your plans. But I'm learning that sometimes, God uses our disruptions to cause us to pray and enter that place that brings deliverance. That means our response matters, even in the inconvenient moments of life. Our perseverance and persistence in prayer, especially in our hopeless moments, are actually a way we can bring glory to God and cause Him to rescue you.

THE PLACE OF PRAYER

It is in the dark spots of our life's situations, in the disruptions to our best plans, we have a choice to either complain or pray about it. Will you be found praying?

Before I bring this chapter to a close, I must bring up one more thing about the place of deliverance. According to the definitions of deliverance, one of those definitions is "giving birth." Therefore, I must say something to those of you who are pregnant with purpose, pregnant with possibilities, pregnant with ministry and etc.; prayer is the place of delivery. It is in this place what prayer calms fears. It is in this place where prayer eases your labor pains. It is in this place where prayer becomes the midwife, and you give birth. Whatever you are pregnant with, now is the time to pray like you never have before. It is prayer that brings that thing, that person, that situation, that you have sweated, worried, or labored over to a place of delivery. Prayer makes your wait less, your want more, and your love deeper for what you are about to give birth to.

CHAPTER 10
A PLACE OF FAITH

Mark 11:22-24 (NLT) Then Jesus said to the disciples, "Have faith in God. I tell you the truth, you can say to this mountain, 'May you be lifted up and thrown into the sea,' and it will happen. But you must really believe it will happen and have no doubt in your heart. I tell you, you can pray for anything, and if you believe that you've received it, it will be yours.

Earlier in this book, in Chapter 3: The Place of Submission, I talked about praying in faith. However, not only should we pray in faith but the act of prayer itself is an act of faith. Faith and Prayer are inseparable. If we have faith that God is sovereign, that He cares for us and loves to communicate with us, we will pray. As a matter of fact, why would you pray if you don't believe that our amazing, omnipotent God can't or won't answer what we are praying for? Therefore, we pray believing that it is already done.

I am aware that there are people who are trying prayer out and there are some that pray just because they have been told that prayer works. However, as a believer and better yet as an intercessor, we pray believing that what we prayed for is already done. Therefore, the act of prayer is the place of faith. Faith is the prerequisite for prayer. At its core, to pray is faith in action. Faith is the confident assurance in the character and promises of God, even when circumstances seem contrary. When Jesus addressed the subject of prayer, He emphasized the importance of faith. Jesus said in

Matthew 21:22 (NKJV) "And whatever things you ask in prayer, believing, you will receive."

This verse underscores that faith is an indispensable and effective component of prayer. Therefore, with prayer being faith in action, the prayer then is trusting that God is able. Not only is He able, but He is able to do more than we can ask or imagine.

The Place of Faith through Prayer

The place of faith through prayer is trusting that God hears our prayers and that He inclines His ear toward us ready to answer our requests. It is also trusting that God is Sovereign and that He knows all things, sees all things, and if He says "no," it is because His ways are infinitely higher than ours. Another thing that the Place of Faith through prayer reminds us is that God loves us as His children and there is nothing and no one that can stand in the way of His plans and purposes for us. After all, He will pick up and throw a mountain into the sea just for us.

In our opening scripture in the book of Mark, I believe that in these verses Jesus invites us to pray with confidence that all things remain possible for our God. No request is ever too great. No need is beyond the reach of God's ability. Therefore, by saying "Have faith in God," Jesus is saying that the outcome of our prayers depends entirely on God. The outcome of our prayers does not depend on our ability to have strong "faith." However, the act of prayer in itself is "faith."

Believe You Received It

You cannot believe that you received it although you don't have it yet without operating through the Holy Spirit in the dimension of faith that is not in the flesh. How do you believe that you receive it? Notice what the NLT says, "…if you believe that you've received it, it will be yours." Therefore, how do you receive something you don't have? If you receive it in one dimension, you will have it in another. So therefore, you can't expect to have it in the natural if you haven't received it in the Spirit. Faith reaches into another realm.

> **WHEN PRAYER AND FAITH COLLIDE, IT PUTS YOU IN THE REALM OF THE SUPERNATURAL.**

We must remember that "PRAYER IS THE KEY BUT FAITH UNLOCKS THE DOOR." Therefore, your place of faith through prayer is rooted in God and His Word. The place of faith through prayer is knowing God's Will, praying it, believing it, and receiving it from Him.

> **FAITH CANNOT GROW OUTSIDE OF THE ENVIRONMENT OF PRAYER. PRAYER IS ITS NATURAL HABITAT.**

~ J. C. P. COCKERTON

Friends, the place of prayer is the place of faith. It demonstrates that we are totally dependent upon God and that we trust Him. We must also remember that prayer is the act that categorically expresses our absolute dependence upon the Lord. It is faith in action.

THE PLACE OF PRAYER

In conclusion, prayer has many places within it. Prayer, in its simplest form, is the way we express our relationship with God. It is communication between us and God, it is walking with God. Prayer is the act that expresses our absolute dependence upon the Lord. Prayer can arise at a time of extreme emotion when we are so overwhelmed that we pour out our hearts to Him. At the same time, prayer can also be a simple moment of awe and thankfulness. Since I am from Kansas, I must make reference to Judy Garland who played Dorothy in the 1939 classic film, "The Wizard of Oz." As she clicked her heels and hoped for the return to the comforts of her own bed and her beloved Auntie Em and Uncle Henry, she said, "There's no place like home." I must leave you with this.

THERE'S NO PLACE LIKE PRAYER.

ABOUT THE AUTHOR
SAMUEL D. ABBOTT, TH. D., M. C.A, B. P. TH.

Bishop, Dr. Samuel D. Abbott began his life in Topeka, Kansas. He was truly anointed and ordained from his mother's womb. He is the son of Hannah and Melvin Abbott. Dr. Abbott attended Kansas City Community College and then Washburn University, majoring in Music Education and then Business management. While at Washburn, Dr. Abbott won the Null Speak-Off competition and scholarship. He was also the president of BSU and started Our Voices Gospel Choir. While attending Abundance of Life COGIC, where his mother was the charter member, under at that time Supt. M.P. Jackson Jr. (who later became the Bishop), Dr. Abbott accepted his calling to the ministry and licensed as a minister in the COGIC. Dr. Abbott went on to earn a Bachelors in Pastoral Theology, a Masters in Christian Administration, and a Doctorate in Theology with emphasis in Leadership all from Faith Bible College of Independence, MO. In 2021, Dr. Abbott received his certification of authorization from The Trauma Healing Institute as an Apprentice in Classic Trauma Healing and now working on his Masters in the same. Dr. Abbott is an entrepreneur. He and Lady Hope own Abbott Solutions LLC. and Hope Academy of Leaders (a K- 8 private school). Dr. Abbott is the dynamically anointed Founder and Senior Pastor of Kingdom Life International founded in Topeka, KS now headquartered in Wichita Falls, TX. Dr. Abbott was ascended to the office of Apostle on August

THE PLACE OF PRAYER

9, 2014, and later consecrated Bishop June 2, 2018. He is the Lead Apostle and Presiding Bishop of the Global Network of Kingdom Ambassadors, which provides spiritual covering and apostolic oversite for ministries, churches, fellowships, and businesses from all over the globe. Dr. Abbott is blessed abundantly to be joined in ministry by his gifted and lovely wife, Hope, one son Raymond, one son in-love; Stacy, three beautiful daughters, Janet, Ara, and Desiree with one daughter-in-love Daina; four beautiful granddaughters, Faith, Sy'Mara, Isabella, and Talayah; also, two Grandsons, Matthias, and Josiah. Dr. Abbott truly walks in an apostolic anointing. He has been called by God to Advance the Kingdom of God, Build Bridges, Carry the Cross Over and Develop Disciples while unifying the Body of Christ and declaring Jesus is Lord! Dr. Abbott carries an empowering presence that creates a life-changing atmosphere where God's Word is confirmed with signs, wonders, and miracles.

You can contact
Dr. Abbott at Bishopsda@mykingdomlife.org.

Made in the USA
Middletown, DE
17 May 2024